I0436788

HATHERILLISMS

Philosophies for Living

by

Dr. David Hatherill

authorHOUSE®

AuthorHouse™
1663 Liberty Drive, Suite 200
Bloomington, IN 47403
www.authorhouse.com
Phone: 1-800-839-8640

© *2008 Dr. David Hatherill. All rights reserved.*

No part of this book may be reproduced, stored in a retrieval system, or transmitted by any means without the written permission of the author.

First published by AuthorHouse 9/3/2008

ISBN: 978-1-4343-3491-6 (e)
ISBN: 978-1-4343-3493-0 (sc)

Library of Congress Control Number: 2007906411

Printed in the United States of America
Bloomington, Indiana

This book is printed on acid-free paper.

Acknowledgments

Thanks to everyone who has ever entered my life in any way, shape, or form whether it was enjoyable or uncomfortable as the culmination of those experiences added to the growth and evolution of who I am now.

Working on yourself never ends.

CONTENTS

Introduction

Welcome to the planet, now prepare to grow! It's up to you! Change the way you approach your life daily and your daily life changes will begin to take your life in a new direction!

Your psychological and your emotional health can change by living with a brighter philosophy for life and a willingness to learn from new perspectives. Accept it, deal with it, and learn to grow from it! It's time to quit complaining and start moving toward a richer life. I have created a book to help you daily. These brief realities keep people connected with the truth.

It's best to read each verse and then relate it to how you can apply it to your daily life. It's not so much what happens with each experience, it's how you react and handle each situation.

My hope in writing this book is that people will see life a little differently and as a result have more productivity, peace, and harmony in their lives.

Use the world as a tool to gain clarity about yourself and others. Learn how to let the world tell you what you need to work on in order to grow.

Once you learn—be prepared to teach. Many opportunities will present themselves from these experiences. Our planet, with all its lessons, is your classroom.

The next time you avoid doing something for fear of failure, remember this: You fail 100% of the time when you don't try!

CHAPTER 1

Wisdoms

1. Personal loans are an investment in seeing who people really are; it's not just about the money.

2. I am not vested in being right, I am vested in knowing the truth.

3. Just because one is not aware of something doesn't mean it doesn't affect them.

4. Just because one is intelligent doesn't mean that they are wise or mentally healthy.

5.   Beauty is as beauty does.

6.   It is amazing how people who are gentle, calm, caring, honest, fun, and sensitive become very attractive.

7.   Just because it was said, doesn't make it so . . . regardless of who said it. Explore or gather information.

8.   Anyone that suggests their ideology is absolute and other ideology is completely invalid—has a need to control. One uses fear as a tool to control.

9.   Taking care of oneself is to believe based on certain realities. It's romantic to blindly believe.

10.   Be extra careful of people who have nothing to lose.

11.   The wisest person I ever met was an 85-year-old woman with an eighth grade education.

12.   Exaggerated actions are often fueled by guilt.

13.   What's most significant may not be what's fair, but it will be reality and something that needs to be dealt with. Complaining about fairness stops you from dealing with the situation. Be more competent when dealing with unfairness.

14. When it comes to knowledge, I'd rather have it and not need it versus need it and not have it.

15. It's not about the mistakes you make, but what wisdom you gain as a result and what you do with it. It's about the wisdom you gained and how you use it.

16. Don't focus on "feeling" at peace, focus on "being" at peace. It's about being a better person as a result.

17. Don't let the role or a title be a smoke screen for the truth.

18. Blame does not heal; it only hurts.

19. Don't be afraid of knowledge. Just because two schools of thought differ doesn't mean it wouldn't be a good idea to explore both.

20. Luck tends to follow skill, knowledge, and tenacity.

21. Those that seek out knowledge, rather than power, become the most powerful in the end.

22. Everyone has something to offer. Be receptive to see if there is something to learn.

23.   Words are like stones, be careful where you throw them.

24.   Sometimes words create wounds that never heal.

25.   Mankind is full of knowledge but starving for wisdom.

26.   A committee of one makes for short meetings.

27.   Instead of being so concerned about the color of someone's skin, be more concerned about the color of someone's character.

28.   Expectations lead to let-downs.

29.   Everyone is one disaster away from poverty, so, don't get cocky.

30.   Equal or unequal is based on how one can benefit. This is the belief in which most people function and this is a problem.

31.   Being honest doesn't necessarily go with being liked.

32.   "We" are "they" and "they" are "we." We have more in common than we have in difference.

33. About cruise ships: I don't like going to a party that I can't leave.

34. One way to heal yourself is to help others.

35. The more one gets, the more one wants, it's human nature. Budget your wants and you'll be more appreciative of what you have.

36. If I treat everyone the same, then I treat no one special. If I treat everybody the same, then how is anyone to know when they are special?

37. "Was" is not "is." Be clear about what no longer exists and know when it's time to move forward with your life.

38. When you make people hungry for information, they are receptive to what you have to say—nobody likes to be told they should or shouldn't be doing something.

39. In the end, one often thinks about the beginning.

40. Forgiveness doesn't mean that things return to the way they were. It has to do with no longer carrying around the anger and resentment that is so damaging to you. The relationship might not return to what it once was, depending on the circumstances.

For example, if someone is caught stealing from me, it wouldn't be prudent to continue allowing them to be in charge of my money. I will forgive them because to not do so takes a toll on me emotionally and physically. I've noticed that many people treat acquaintances better and with more respect than those they call friends or even supposedly love.

41. Forgive and remember...to forget usually leads to a repeat of the same . . . to accept doesn't mean that you agree. It means that you see the truth then make adjustments based on the acceptance of the facts of the situation. Then deciding what's the healthiest way to take care of yourself while not holding onto any resentment or anger which only harms yourself.

42. Often, being right is not enough.

43. If you want someone to see something, take them to it.

44. Understanding and appreciating the hard work and sacrifices of those before you will keep you humble and clear about your abilities.

45. Most writings of ancient days can be applied today.

46. Sometimes the best teachers aren't the most gifted.

CHAPTER 2

Personal Growth

1.   When you see someone being critical of others, you are looking at someone who is avoiding themselves.

2.   The act of putting down someone only takes a moment; the act of being a better person takes more time, commitment, and energy. Secure people don't go around putting down other people and are more likely to help while having compassion.

3.   People who put down others are showing their own insecurities. By putting down others, they are making themselves feel bigger.

4.   Be open to see what the world is telling you that "you need to work on." This message often comes in the form of the discomfort of not getting what you want.

5.   It is not what happens that is as significant as how one grows from the experience.

6.   Change some of the ways you approach living and your life changes.

7.   You need to make changes in you not just outside of you if you want your life to change. Many of these changes may feel uncomfortable.

8.   Learn to appreciate the discomfort life provides because that is where the opportunity for growth is, then discomfort is not so bad.

9.   Refusing to listen to how others experience you is a commitment to staying the same; there is no opportunity for growth when you are not willing to look at yourself.

10.   Who promised that heaven will always feel good? If there is more growth to be done, don't count on always feeling good!

11.   Without adversity, we stay the same or dwindle to become even less.

12.   Make your goal in life to grow from the discomfort in situations you are experiencing rather than to feel better. As you will grow, you will feel better. A bi-product of growth is that you often feel better. Because feeling better is a measure of "being" more competent to deal with living when your feelings are connected to reality, but if not, they distort reality. Just because you feel like people are angry at you doesn't mean that they are.

13.   Life is about change. Sometimes it hurts; sometimes it feels good. The sooner you learn to accept it in your life, the faster you will be able to turn the change into growth and the less stressful life will be.

14.   You get what you give. If you don't agree with this then perhaps you have been trading not giving, expecting something in return.

15.   As a result of crisis, you have a choice to transform into being bitter or being better. A person's real self surfaces in crisis.

16.   What harmful things/deeds one did in the past doesn't mean that you're necessarily an evil person. It's very important that one can see the harm they did and do what

is needed to repair or correct it. Additionally, one must recognize how to never commit the same behavior. This step provides that learning and growth has happened.

17.   If I had the ability to put you on an island where you had absolutely everything you wanted, nothing but fun and no uncomfortable challenges—after 10 years you would be very much the same. But if I put you on an island where you were presented with many different painful challenges to overcome, then after 10 years you would be very different. You would be more competent to handle the obstacles life provided. You would be more of a person than you were; better able to be a friend, teacher, helper, family member, parent, etc. Well, welcome to the planet Earth.

18.   Stopping people from experiencing the consequences of their behavior or choices doesn't always help them. Sometimes the only way for someone to learn and grow is to not protect them from harm or discomfort.

19.   What did I hear? "Not me?" Is that defensiveness? Remember, defensiveness stops you from looking at yourself which is what is needed for growth. Defensiveness keeps you the same.

20.   If you were in a perfect world, you would be on another planet. Quit wasting valuable time whining about how

unfair life is. Life is often unfair if one is coming from the position of getting and/or wanting more.

21. Life is sequential. When you regret previous circumstances or events, it is valuable to remember that you would not be who you are if it were not for those events. So find value in what happens to you in life.

22. When I am not honestly being myself, I am moving farther away from growing to be better.

23. We see as we are, not as it is. This is how "our" beliefs, thoughts and feelings often distort reality.

24. Knowing when something has nothing to do with you is very freeing. It allows you not to get caught up in or over-react to or become reactive or feel responsible for other people's unresolved stuff. And when it does have something to do with you, then you deal with it. Remember, very seldom is anything personal. You just happen to be there.

25. How others judge is of no importance to a secure person. That doesn't mean one has to tolerate rude behavior.

26. When confronted with difference, who we are is magnified.

27.   When one tries to control something that they have no power over, they become out of control.

28.   When someone says, "Hi, how are you?" The insightful response would be: "Well, all my body parts are working and I am at peace, so I am doing just fine."

29.   When you are watching a movie and you notice that you are experiencing a strong feeling then look at the theme of that scene. That will tell you something about yourself. Remember, your focus is to be on what emotion is going on in you, not so much about if the movie is good or not. It's using the movie as a tool to gain clarity about what moves you. It can help give you some insight with regard to what moves you.

30.   With regard to different lifestyles: Most can work if you work at it and have good intentions.

31.   I would rather be taller in stature than in inches.

32.   Many people live out their lives playing a role and have no idea who they really are. Work more on being real versus living a role.

33.   Ask someone who they are, and they'll usually refer to a role, such as doctor or artist, mother or student, when

that's not really who they are. Remember, wherever you go, there you are.

34. Self-esteem and self-image are different but related. Self-esteem is your ability to cope with or be competent at dealing with life, regardless of how you feel. Self-image is the way you see and feel about yourself.

35. Don't conclude that because someone has wealth or fame that they also have wisdom or maturity.

36. Years ago I remember saying the phrase, "I wish I knew then what I know now." And now I realize how little I knew then.

37. Instead of wishing—set out a plan for doing. You are going to get older, so you might as well become wiser along the way.

38. Don't be one of those people who ends up just getting older, work on "being" better not just "feeling" better.

39. If you are not happy with the people you are attracting, don't blame them; rather, look at yourself.

40. You can learn much by just observing. Remember, observe without judgment. If you want to learn about frogs you

need to sit and observe frogs. You wouldn't say, "Oh, what a stupid thing that frog did," because that's judging and it detracts from learning about frogs. Similarly, if you want to learn about yourself, study your own behavior without judgment. The same applies to others as well.

41. Try to remember when it comes to "meeting needs," we humans have more in common than we have differences. We just have unique ways of acting out.

42. Be open to seeing "what is" rather than what you "want" to see. Stop running from yourself. Relationships act as mirrors. They make us look at ourselves. So, work on liking what you see.

43. The next time you find yourself complaining that someone is weird, just think how boring it would be if everyone were exactly like you.

44. People are like musical instruments. Stay in tune and the music you play will sound so much better.

45. It is not good for you to be distrustful of everyone. On the other hand, it's just not good judgment to think everyone is trustworthy.

46. The older I get the longer it takes to recover from just about everything.

47. People are generally attracted to what they value.

48. Many believe that we are what we do, but what we think and value dictates what we do . . . what we do is only evidence to suggest who we are. Don't come to huge conclusions with a small amount of information. If you do, you will distort the truth.

49. Know yourself no matter what body you are driving. My body is the vehicle by which I get around in.

50. Learn to live in harmony with your body/mind; enjoy them, get to know them, and treat them well.

51. We all beat up people in our own way; this includes ourselves.

52. The things, people, and events we grow up with become a part of us. After all, part of who we are is the experiences that we take with us.

53. There's much more to see, but we really don't want to see it. Denial is bliss until the truth surfaces.

54. The phrase *Have no fear* is not always connected to reality. Fear is often an indicator that you might be in danger and something needs to be done.

55.   Unhappiness is best defined as the difference between one's distorted self-image and reality of who they really are, which explains why they don't get what they feel they deserve. Unhappy people don't appreciate what is being offered.

56.   There are a number of people who are liars. The sooner you accept this fact the more likely it is that you will be able to see who is and who is not. Denial is not a safe place to be. Rose colored glasses can lead to black eyes.

57.   Avoidance doesn't lead to calmness, but rather to underlying anxiety that builds as time goes by.

58.   Don't confuse attention with respect. How you get the attention makes a difference.

59.   If only I had a quarter for every want I've ever had, I'd be so busy counting them that I would be distracted from actually living.

60.   When one is all about entitlement, one lives a life of frustration and disappointments. And one is usually a pain in the !@#$&* to others!

61.   All true tests in life come down to not relying on others.

62. To apply myself to living is to live as it applies.

63. When I'm not honestly being myself, I'm moving farther away from growing to be better.

64. If you want a better self-image and self-esteem then you must be willing to look at yourself with brutal honesty and work on the areas that need improvement.

65. When you are clear about who you are, what you need to do is a given.

66. In general, in society, people are judged by their role rather than who they really are. And in general, people are blinded by roles.

67. Ask yourself: Is the way I am seen, the way I am? And, do I want to do anything about it?

68. What is your reaction to not being able to control someone you want to control? How you answer this reveals much of what you need to work on in you.

69. Remember, they are not you and you are not them. People don't think, feel, or respond in the same ways. So, do yourself a favor and quit expecting others to be like you . . . difference is what makes the world interesting.

70. Life is the best therapist. You need to learn how to hear and listen to what is being said.

71. Just because people can be rehabilitated doesn't mean that they are ready and willing. It is important to notice if people want your help.

72. If you can't be entertained by real life, then you are not very entertaining.

73. Having a license to "do" something doesn't guarantee that one is good at what it is they are licensed to do. But, it is at least a guarantee that they were given the training and passed what a state governing board (usually the board of consumer affairs) decided were the necessary educational requirements and training required to protect the public from harm. If one is not licensed to provide professional service, they are likely working around the law, which is usually not in your best interest; no matter what the service is. When seeking any kind of service ask if they have a license to practice that service.

74. Feelings can give clarity when they are connected to reality. It is unwise to make choices based on feelings alone without first doing a reality check.

75. When feelings are attached to reality, people have the opportunity to learn about themselves via uncomfortable feelings.

76. Defensiveness is the #1 killer of personal growth.

77. To lend a friend money? Bad judgment? Not necessarily. It's an opportunity to gain clarity about who they are. You risk not only losing money, but losing a concept about them that may not be true. Don't lend more than you can afford to lose. You pay for education, how much are you willing to invest?

78. The ability to feel is just that, the ability to feel. You can't expect to only feel joy and pleasure without the ability to feel sorrow and pain. Be competent at experiencing both.

79. Wanting too much is the pathway to sorrow. Spending more time valuing what you have leads to contentment. You can still continue to achieve, it's just a happier way of going about it.

80. To really value life, experience what it's like to almost die! (I am not suggesting this, but rather I am making a point!)

81.   The idea that I should be something I'm not prevents me from seeing who I am. I need to understand who I am in order to improve.

82.   It's often when situations are ending that we think about what created the beginning.

83.   When a man is very sick and in the care of a nurturing woman, he becomes the little boy he once was and she becomes his mother.

84.   Someone who has experienced abuse in the past may be easily upset by yelling versus someone who comes from a cultural background where high volume and animated dialogue is standard practice.

85.   Get professional help where abuse was involved because past abuse leads to present patterns of abuse, including self-abuse. Seek out licensed professional help if you have a history of emotional, psychological, or physical abuse.

86.   People focus more often on what they don't have rather than what they do have. Appreciate what is being offered and you will be more content.

87. Every car needs a generator or alternator and every human being needs to have some fun. Don't forget to recharge your system by having fun.

88. Ask yourself: "What needs to be different in my life that would cause me to take better care of myself?"

89. Some people treat their cars better than they do their own bodies. Both are for transportation, but one can't be replaced. Take care of yourself.

90. I don't understand *it*, but I am against *it*. This position keeps one ignorant.

91. Being "in" with the "in crowd" is completely based on one's judgment of who exactly the "in crowd" is.

92. Ask yourself how often you do things that are not good for you and whether you are okay with continuing to do these things. If the answer is yes then it would be a good idea to remember that we take care of the things that we value.

93. Self-esteem is not how one feels about him- or herself. It's how competent one is at dealing with what life dishes out. How you feel about yourself is about self-image.

94. I am prejudice. But it's not against skin color, religion, language, or what country they are coming from. I am prejudiced against people with bad manners. So, if I don't want to be around you, don't blame it on anything other than your behavior. Stop making up excuses for being a jerk. Stop using other reasons to justify continuing to act like a jerk.

95. It has been my experience that traditional manners are the best. After all, they have been around longer and therefore have had more time to be perfected.

96. Did you ever consider that maybe the reason that I came to the beach was to listen to the sound of the waves instead of being forced to listen to the sound of another person's music? Use headphones in public places and have respect for others.

97. I'll bet you that every handicapped person on the planet who can't walk would gladly trade you his or her handicapped parking permit for your ability to walk. I would bet they would eagerly park far away from the store, even if it meant walking an extra mile to get to the store everyday, just for the opportunity to be able to walk using their own legs. So, don't park in the handicapped parking or complain that there is too much of it. Enjoy your walk. You may not always be able to. The best way

to celebrate what you have is to use what you have. Don't take it for granted!

98. Everyone can sing. I just happen to be someone who can't sing in key. I enjoy singing just the same. Just because I like to sing doesn't mean that others want to listen to me as I sing along with the radio.

99. There have been times when people have gotten a wrong impression of me. They have taken a brief experience with me and drawn big conclusions from it. That's where the distortion of me begins. My contribution is that I sometimes forget that people do this, and when I say or do something without taking into consideration how another may misunderstand what I am doing; and without more information about me this could be misleading.

100. Think about what the implied message might be to others before you say what you want to say. You may change your mind about saying it.

101. When one values furniture more than making people feel comfortable, one runs the risk of having a house full of only furniture. Focus on making people feel comfortable and welcome then one will always have people in their life.

102. Don't force your kids on others. Parent your kids at all times, especially when you are in public. Some people choose not to have children, and they don't want to be put into the position of having to parent yours.

103. If you make a promise to someone do your best to follow through, not only when it is convenient to do so. The reputation you build will pay off big in the long run.

104. The practice of bad manners by others is a "pop quiz" for you to see how much you have learned about dealing with people who have bad manners.

105. They are wearing their Sunday best. Why don't we live with these principles anymore? The way we dress shows respect or disrespect. Casual isn't necessarily friendly, in fact, casual can be bad-manners and bad-manners are never friendly!

106. To be a good teacher you must first be a good student. When you understand what is needed to be learned, you begin to understand what is needed in order to teach.

107. Treat people as they deserve to be treated based on who they are and not to be confused with other people who are similar.

108. Coming to conclusions too soon with little facts to support them is a dangerous habit. It's the beginning of prejudice and distortions of reality. First impressions are usually first conclusions. Coming to conclusions too soon often leads to being wrong about people.

109. Better to be a "has been" than a "never will be."

110. Maturity is more about having good manners, rather than being intelligent or formally educated. And, maturity rests on the shoulders of how one handles disappointments.

111. The only way to have true objectivity is to not care about the results.

112. We are constantly being given "pop quizzes." They present to us in the form of the options we have and the choices we make. These reveal much of who we are.

113. When you allow money to dictate ethics, then you become worthless.

114. How are you helping the less fortunate when your involvement costs them more than they benefit? Are you hiding behind the false claim of "helping" when in fact you are taking advantage? Will your intervention do more to hinder than to help? Many professions would

change their approaches if they looked honestly at their interventions through these glasses.

115. You don't have to be in a building to be locked in jail. Many people take their jail with them. Your job is to find the key that will set you free. And, recognize who your jailers are in your life. Then do what's needed to set yourself free to be who you really are.

116. Tenacity without careful planning and insight (foresight) can be reckless and destructive. Careful planning without tenacity can lead to many unfinished projects.

117. You need insight with tenacity because insight is needed to make adjustments along the way. Foresight is needed to make sure adjustments made are consistent with ultimate goals.

118. Make choices based on "what is" versus "what if." How often do "what ifs" really happen?

119. When given training and education, people discover that they can do things they didn't think they could do before; this creates motivation.

120. Practice doesn't make perfect. Practicing perfect technique makes perfect. Practicing poor technique means you become good at playing poorly.

121. Where the mind is dictates the action. So, keep your mind straight.

122. Like a drink of cold water to a thirsty person, it's refreshing to hear when people "see" the truth, especially when most choose to ignore or cannot see the truth for themselves because their opinions get in the way.

123. A psychotherapist's job is to move people to see the truth about themselves and others and then help them to become competent at dealing with the truth in a way that facilitates emotional and psychological growth.

124. Many of us doctors think we know everything just because we know a lot about one thing.

125. People try to rationalize evil as caused by something or someone else. Evil is often attached to receiving pain and discomfort and not getting what one wants at a time when it appears to be given unjustly and without consideration of providing what someone feels they are entitled to receive based on their subjective deeds.

126. To live within the walls of "wanting" something lost that you can't regain is a painful prison to live in.

127. "There may be some truth to what's being said." Looking at things this way is your opportunity to grow.

128. Remember, what you are going through has value for your growth.

129. The areas one needs to work on shows in the repeated problems one has in their life.

CHAPTER 3

Goals & Aspirations

1. When I am the first one to know or see, then the opportunities lie with me.

2. Oh, to be a champion! To be the best at anything at any point in time, for any length of time, is a moment that lasts forever.

3. Be less committed to getting more; be more committed to being more. Your life will work better.

4. The best revenge is to be successful!

5.   Revenge is a form of justice one is not supposed to enjoy but where satisfaction is often found.

6.   We often judge ourselves by what we feel we are capable of doing rather than noticing the fact of what we are really capable of doing. No wonder we often get ourselves in over our head.

7.   We often want our lives to be something different rather than noticing and valuing what it is.

8.   I'd probably get somewhere if I quit saying, "what if" and based my choices on reality.

9.   What you want to do may not be exactly what you are meant to do. Pay attention to what direction the world seems to be moving you. Sometimes it's just a matter of paying your dues before you get your turn to do what you want. And sometimes, it's a matter of taking pride in doing the best you can at what you were meant to do and seeing the value in doing it.

10.   To help you cope with loss and situations ending that you wish would continue, remember that in order to experience new beginnings one must have endings.

11.   One has no more dreams when they have everything. Then, one has nothing more to look forward to. So,

therefore, please God don't ever give me everything I want so that I may always have something to strive for and to look forward to.

12.   You have been able to deal with the reality and receptive to seeing what the truth is.

13.   What one is generally interested in is what they excel at, even if aptitude tests state otherwise.

14.   Self-esteem is the competence to be able to cope with what life dishes out.

15.   When you blame, you give control to external circumstances. It's healthier to look at what you don't have control over and work on accepting this and focus on what you have some degree of control over. Make a plan of action and get started. Look at your degree of contribution and don't blame others. This is where you have opportunity for personal growth.

Blame removes the opportunities to take control and you will stay the same. Focusing on not having control leads to two components of depression: Helplessness and hopelessness.

16.   The only thing over which you really have or will ever have any degree of true ownership of is your life. Anything else

that you may think you own is, in reality, only borrowed, rented, or reserved until you die. So, what are you going to do with your life? Are you satisfied with what you have done with it? If not, what are you going to do about it and when?

Life does not last forever on this planet, and without warning, it could end any day. Your life is the only thing you can take with you when you die.

17. Deadlines can influence life lines.

18. Make deadlines a part of your life and your life will have a better chance of succeeding.

19. Dream with a deadline and your dreams will have a better chance of becoming reality.

20. When you are the worst at something that means you are the best at being the worst at something . . . it is all in the way you look at things.

21. I've noticed that many elderly people tend to look at only what they cannot do at this point in their lives. They compare what they are capable of doing at this point in time in their life with what they used to be able to do and feel worthless as a result. Just because you can no longer

do the things you used to do does not detract from the value and contributions of those accomplishments.

I want to remind you all that if it were not for the older generation's sacrifices over the years, the generations that have followed would not have the great opportunities this country offers. There is much for you to be proud of. On behalf of those of us from a younger generation, I thank you for all that you have done. Your past accomplishments will always be a part of who you are and can never be taken away from you. Be proud of what you have done. Who you are is a compilation of your past experiences. Acknowledge your cumulative deeds of worth and value and you may feel better about yourself.

22. Life and growth are a process. Work on being in better condition to deal with all areas of life. Exercise to be better prepared to address each situation as it occurs.

23. People often blur the line between fact and opinion and become defensive when you try to point it out. They may be so attached to their opinions that they actually confuse opinion with fact or reality.

24. Sometimes one's self-worth is wrapped up in the idea that one can possess the ability to save everyone. When these intentions fail the result is often that good intentions cause greater harm within the situation. Many times one

is so self-involved in the grand "do-gooder delusion" that one becomes convinced that the events leading up to their interference and resulting disaster did not happen exactly the way they did.

In an effort to avoid taking responsibility, one can rewrite history and describe the series of events in such a way as to bring relief from any guilt or blame. One can truly believe this distorted version of events. Even if no one else agrees with him (denial).

25. When we become adults we sometimes are able to see our parents outside of their roles as mothers and fathers. When you can do this, you may be ready to see them for the very first time in your life as they truly are.

26. Look for the compliments in what people say. You may be surprised at all the compliments that you never heard before.

27. The phrase "wasting time" is very subjective. Watch those judgments, folks. Many creative ideas have come from people who others saw as wasting time.

28. Is it preferred to finish last in a group of the best versus best in a group of the worst?

29. The phrase, "You can have anything you want if you want it bad enough and are willing to work hard enough to get it" represents the American way, but it's not true. The United States is the greatest country for opportunity, but you need to be realistic. Be open to compromises and modifications. Just because I want to play professional basketball doesn't mean it is possible, no matter how hard I work. Be more attached to your capabilities.

30. In order to learn, grow, and gain wisdom, don't limit yourself to listening to educated people. For instance, homeless people have experiences that may reveal secrets to understanding this world that an educated professor may not be able to offer.

31. Often our best teachers surprise us by disguising themselves as people who are not qualified to provide us with insight on life.

32. A person who believes he already knows a great number of things often in reality has a lot to learn, but rarely does because he is too attached to his own opinions and cannot remain receptive to learning from experiences. He or she thinks they know it all and are therefore not receptive to new ideas, information, or knowledge.

33. What better way to learn patience than from someone who tries your patience?

34. You will find more value in living when you develop the philosophy to learn and grow from everything that you encounter.

35. Be careful when listening to psychics. I'm not saying there aren't people out there who have psychic abilities, but the information they provide may be incomplete. You can make some very poor choices with incomplete information.

36. As my dad once said, I may not have an answer for your questions now, but give me some time and I will have an answer for you.

37. If we manage our stress level more like most people manage their money, we would cope better with stressors. You wouldn't spend $20 of emotion on a $1 issue. It is called emotional budgeting.

38. Sex is a wonderful gift that we have been given. Enjoy it. Don't feel guilty about it. In the right context, sex is wonderful, but like anything it can be misused.

39. Life presents pop quizzes in the form of situations we didn't prepare for. How we deal with them tells us how we're doing and whether we are ready to learn and what we need to learn.

40. Knowing other languages is the key to opening many doors to experiencing more of what the world has to offer. When you speak in another language, it forces you to see life just a little bit differently.

41. Knowing other languages allows one to more fully experience other customs and cultures and travel as a participant rather than an outside observer.

42. Don't make decisions in your life based on other people's judgments.

43. Make listening a habit and you will have more to say when it's your turn to talk.

44. Wisdom and knowledge come from those who are open to it.

45. Often people confuse acting with being.

46. One cannot become wise by arguing and refusing to see experience from other people. True learning comes from exploring what others are saying. Exploring not arguing.

47. Don't be so attached to your beliefs that you aren't open to new information.

48. Do you argue or become defensive when presented with new information? You may be more attached to your opinions than you think.

49. Don't be so hasty to defend your opinions—you might miss an opportunity to learn something.

50. People have moments of being out of control. How often and to what degree depends on the amount of unresolved psychological issues.

51. Value reading as it is an important learning tool. You have access to just about any information you desire in the library and on the Internet.

52. Allow creativity to come to you, and make room for it. It is not something you can force.

53. In some cultures the word "should" does not exist. People either "do" or "they don't" and then they deal with "what is" as a result. "Should" doesn't have any relevance to what actually is or isn't happening. The very use of the word means the situation doesn't exist.

54. Learning to play a musical instrument will get you more in tune with the flow of life.

55. Things are not good or bad. It is what we do with them that make them harmful or helpful. Quit blaming inanimate objects and external situations. Take responsibility for your choices, actions, and behaviors. Look at your degree of contribution to outcomes.

56. Study and practice love and you will get better at it. How can you do something well if you don't understand it?

57. Look for opportunities to help others. The universe will treat you better.

58. Live where you play. Then, when you get home, you don't have to go anywhere to have fun.

59. In society the bottom line is it's what you "DO" that defines you! It's not what you think or what you say or how you feel. It's what you do with how you feel, think, and say. It's about what differences you make as a result of being alive on this planet.

60. Replace "what if" with "what is" and your decisions will be much more reality based.

61. Notice what you do well then acknowledge how much effort it took. Now imagine if you put that much effort into being a healthy, happy, and caring person.

62.   Money increases the odds of being able to help. Notice if you take the opportunity to do so.

63.   If you want to reduce crime, help people get out of poverty.

64.   If you are living from the standpoint of trying to find time, you will seldom find it. When you "make time," then you will have it.

65.   Money does not buy happiness; however, it can eliminate many financial stressors, create more opportunities, and increase the odds for achieving happiness.

66.   If you are going to have a dog, then experience having a dog; otherwise it's not fair to the dog. Life, in general, is the same way.

67.   If you don't contribute to the good of society, then what good are you? If your efforts are only to glorify yourself, you will not be missed. Therefore, selfish acts actually only diminish your existence and by the time you know this, it may be too late to do anything about it. That's what your life is—your chance to be meaningful.

68.   How one dresses says much about that someone. It's often a statement about a position one is taking and/or about how they feel about themselves. Dressing in a manner

that fits in with others is a way of showing respect for others.

69. Good deeds are valued more when discovered by others versus campaigned for.

70. Focus more energy on controlling and changing yourself rather than others and you will be better company and a better person.

71. Instead of looking for a job, look for a lifestyle for making money. This takes into account who you are and not just making money.

72. Continue what you love. If a break is required, set a date to resume.

73. Competition is a good thing as long as you don't take it too seriously. How you approach competition will tell you something about yourself; if you are open to it.

74. There will always be a percentage of poor no matter what society and government do simply because there will always be people who do not have the ability or desire to be successful.

75. Allow for adjustments or needed modifications along the way. Be receptive to verbal feedback from those who have more success and experience than you. Listen to those who have a good track record of success.

76. To be successful one needs top-quality skills, knowledge of what is needed to be successful, and the commitment and tenacity to overcome all obstacles regardless of the level of discomfort one has to experience.

77. The best way to get over the past is to begin something new.

78. Don't let one bad hole in golf ruin the other 17 holes.

79. The best way to value living is to do things of worth and value.

80. After the brain has been doing something for so long a period of time it gets to be harder to change . . . Don't put off growth or it may be too late.

81. To stay on a healthy path: Everyday look at your life honestly. Review to see if what you are doing is growth or health-oriented and compatible with who you are. Make a promise or commitment to live a life of worth and value. Know yourself well and have some general life direction based on who you are. Notice yourself without

judgment but with acceptance and clarify to always be open to get to know yourself better.

82. Often music touches people in ways that words alone cannot.

83. Music comes literally and figuratively from the beat of the heart. How life would be lacking without it.

84. When you wish to say something that is very meaningful, you might consider using music to help.

85. Music has a way of bringing back the past.

86. A lifetime of learning is similar to high school. When you have completed the required course work, you graduate and never go back.

87. In high school my sister Joyce told me, "Enjoy it because it goes by fast and you can never go back to those days." Life here on the planet is the same way. Approach life the same way and you will get more out of it as a result.

88. We can learn much about ourselves by observing other animals. Don't forget that we are primates.

89. I want to say thank you to the universe for all the lessons it has given me, regardless of how painful they were. My visit to the planet has been of great value and I hope there are many more lessons to follow.

90. Some things just are what they are. You don't have to understand them; you just have to accept them.

91. Be careful of making choices based on feelings alone. Feelings often distort reality. For instance, just because I feel like someone doesn't like me doesn't necessarily mean that I am correct.

92. Assumptions based on feelings alone are often inaccurate and disconnected from reality. Before reacting on your emotions, take the time to get a reality check. Tell someone what you are thinking and feeling. Get a second opinion to see if your feelings are appropriate to the situation. Oftentimes, they will not be and you will save yourself from unnecessarily conflict and/or embarrassment.

93. Because it's said, doesn't make it so.

94. The slogan, "Do your own thing," came out of the late 1960s and has been misused and misinterpreted. Often a rude and insensitive person uses this phrase to give himself permission to do and say anything he wants regardless of

how it affects others. Don't look for excuses to be selfish, irresponsible, hurtful, or just plain "bad company."

95. When you focus too much on the end result of the goals you desire, you practice delayed gratification, which can lead to long periods of frustration. When you focus on progress, you experience success on a regular and ongoing basis.

96. An attitude is like a door—it can let in opportunity or lock it out.

97. There is enough discomfort in life without you helping it along.

98. Doing things of worth doesn't mean that you have to save lives or to be president of a company or country. It simply means that when you see an opportunity to be helpful, then help. In those cases when you really can't help, don't worry about it. But when you can, then do. The world will be a little better place to live as a result.

99. A willow tree moves in whichever way the wind blows. If you are like a willow, make sure you are surrounded by strong healthy trees to help protect you or better yet work on being stronger yourself.

100. A life without sadness is a life without wisdom.

101. A legacy is in effect a statement that I was here, so acknowledge me. We all have a need to be acknowledged. At an early age we have all said, "Hey, Mom or Dad, watch me do this!"

102. A good seaman weathers the storm he cannot avoid and avoids the storm he cannot weather. Be honest with yourself about your abilities and you live like the good seaman.

103. A boat cannot sail from the wind that has passed. Increase your awareness so you will see when opportunities are presented.

104. Anger has a way of deflating one's IQ.

105. Do not dwell on one's juvenile offenses especially when most recent adult events are more significant. Look to see who people are now; you may be surprised at the growth that has occurred. Remember wisdom comes from experience not from books. Get away from wishing that certain things never happened.

106. When you don't plan well, you plan to fail.

107. It's not so much the circumstances, it's how you deal with the circumstances.

108. When others give you feedback about something you're doing that bothers them and your reaction to that is to explain it away, what you are really saying with your explanation is that you are more vested in continuing to do things and don't really care much about how it affects the other person.

109. Let's see what is interfering to learn how you can better yourself.

110. Finding your balance-to-lifestyle is a key to healthful, happy living. Not everyone will have the same balance because there are no two people who are exactly the same.

111. How wonderful to be the best in the world at something.

112. To be a person of integrity means having to stand up for what you believe to be "right" even when it creates hardships for you.

113. Nonconformity as a lifestyle is doing things differently than the norm for ego gratification and personal identity. People who practice nonconformity with the intention to force change for the better good of society, and often make great sacrifices in the process, are truly agents for mankind.

CHAPTER 4

Family

1. A statement from an adoptive (or foster) child to their non-biological parent: You have no idea how much of "you" is inside me. I say the things you said. I cope, react, and problem solve just as you did. The genes may not be there, but our life together was deeply significant in the depth of the development of my being who I am.

My experiences growing up with your guidance cumulatively has overridden even genetic predispositions to the point that your guidance and influence on me is now who I am. I see you in my speech, habits, interests, and humor. To say we are not related is simply not true.

2. When someone says to a foster or adopted child: "You're not really related to them," they are demonstrating how little they are able to see who I have become. And they are showing a lack of understanding of how I have become who I am. It is also an insult to my parent. You dismiss all of the hard work and loving attention that my parent gave to me that formed who I am. To say we are not related is like saying that cellular phones are not connected. When one is reared by another, a part of their personality becomes engrained in their character.

3. Before we are allowed to do certain things that can impact others, such as driving a car or carrying a gun, we are required to prove we have sufficiently studied the subject matter, by getting a permit or being licensed. Think about the responsibilities that go along with being a parent, and the fact that most people get no training or education regarding parenting. If you decide to have children, study the art of parenting.

4. It is not always in the best interest of children to give them everything they want.

5. It's common to believe that just because you are related to someone, you are going to like them. Not necessarily so. You are different people, related or not.

6. Children have no control over their family situations. Families are the parents' responsibilities. So whatever happened to you when you were a child, you were not and are not responsible. Do not blame yourself.

7. Families can be the most damaging of entities or the most healing and nurturing of institutions. The responsibilities involved with starting a family are much greater than many people realize.

8. Don't get into physical confrontations with friends, family, or loved ones. Arguments do happen and are sometimes necessary to clear the air. However, only in self-defense is physical violence called for.

9. A thankless child often evolves into a thankless adult.

10. Close families are not without distance.

11. Don't relate so much to the body or genetics when it comes to family. From a strictly spiritual standpoint, our mother is just our portal by which we arrived here on the planet. We are no more or less related to her than one of our close friends or neighbors.

12. In many cases the family is the primary contributing factor to your emotional and psychological dysfunction, so work on being a healthful family member.

13. From "Ow" to "Wow!" When one sees people they love for who they really are rather than who they thought they were.

14. "Dad" or "Mom" is a job description.

15. You have much less choice when it comes to family, but at least you can develop a sense of family with friendship.

CHAPTER 5

Relationships

1. "Come on! Not even you believe your story!" Ask yourself how often this statement has applied; and not only with regard to others. People fool themselves constantly.

2. Others are entitled to be wrong, even if it's about you. Don't get so worked up about it!

3. I've seen many attractive people quickly turn ugly because of the way they behaved toward others and the way they treated others.

4. A partnership is not equal if you are the only one at risk. Putting in equal time and or equal money isn't enough. You need to look at who takes responsibility if circumstances don't go as planned and who will pay the consequences.

5. Look for ways to turn weaknesses into strengths.

6. What one does is good for some and not so good for others.

7. What people find humorous says much about them.

8. What we do with people contributes to the memories of their lives.

9. When you think too much of what others think, you lose your own thought.

10. You really don't know someone until you have had some kind of disagreement with them. Most people are good company when things are going their way.

11. You will know more about someone when they are made executor of a will.

12.   You will know someone better after you have lent money to them. A loan is often an investment as it provides clarification of who that person is. We pay for education.

13.   Masculine versus feminine is not a good or bad thing. It is a reality of nature and we need to acknowledge and enjoy the difference.

14.   People say, "I love you" in different ways. Many of them are nonverbal. Look and listen more closely. Get away from requiring that the statement be done your way.

15.   When trying to help someone, if you notice that you are putting more effort into helping them than they are willing to help themselves then stop.

16.   When people are lacking in emotional growth or the social skills to connect with others, they sometimes use sex to connect with others; there are often problems when people use sex for non-sex needs.

17.   If you don't like the way others act toward you, consider whether they are reacting to something you are doing. When there is a constant negative reaction, chances are you are a contributing factor.

18.   Addiction to people is no different than addiction to drugs or alcohol. Do not confuse addiction with love. A loving relationship is not destructive.

19.   If you begin to see that you never really had a friendship, but rather only a one-sided arrangement, it may be time to reassess what a relationship is. Remember that relationships are based on reciprocation.

20.   Sometimes people grow in different directions, thereby reducing the degree of compatibility. Before you make any final decisions, be clear about what you are giving up.

21.   Replace the phrase, "It's my fault" with "what was my contribution to the outcome?" Fault implies a need for punishment and shame. Using "my contribution" implies having an opportunity to learn and grow from what occurred.

22.   There is nothing wrong with not liking someone's company or not wanting to be around someone. It is natural. It's how one deals with those feelings that makes the difference. We all have the right to not like someone, but we don't have the right to be cruel or aggressive toward them.

23. We all get angry at times. How you react and express that anger determines if there is something you to need to explore about yourself.

24. See if you can grow as a person as a result of working through a conflict. It doesn't always mean that the relationship is going to move forward, but it's worth a try. Remember, when a relationship ends, it's usually gone forever.

25. In order to communicate with a weasel, you need to speak the language a weasel understands. The polite, appropriate style of communication doesn't always work.

26. When someone truly gives, they don't expect anything in return. Their absolute joy is in the act of giving. When you expect something in return you are trading not giving.

27. Remember you can't have it both ways. When you involve yourself in someone's life and it works out great, then you get some of the credit. But when things don't work out, you must also acknowledge your contribution and accept some of the responsibility. You had contribution with your involvement; therefore, own up to it.

28. I once received a phone call from an ex-girlfriend who had made plans for us for an upcoming visit. The only

problem was that she didn't seem to be at all interested in what I thought about her plans or what I wanted to do. It reminded me of why our relationship did not last very long.

29. If you are angry with someone, talk about it. Don't act it out. When you are upset over something, it is not the time to play charades.

30. People cannot read your mind, so quit practicing the silent treatment. Silence can be very loud.

31. I have noticed that when people are in close relationships, often they think that the other person can read their mind. Eliminate the guesswork and talk to each other.

32. When conflicts or disagreements are handled constructively, you can grow closer together. A lack of communication can bring on destructive behavior and exhaust a relationship.

33. Sincerity is flattering. Insincerity is offensive.

34. I'm not a jerk because I called you on your inappropriate behavior. You are a jerk for putting me in a position where I had to.

35. The ability to resolve conflicts is a part of compatibility. Conflict, in and of itself, is not necessarily evidence of incompatibility.

36. Work on being important by growing and hard work, versus just trying to feel better by trying to act smarter or by putting others down.

37. Don't use trying to make someone else lose as a way of gaining reassurances that someone cares for you. You can ruin many an evening trying to measure someone's love for you this way.

38. It amazes me how many people don't pay attention to how others react to their behavior and actions.

39. It is generally a good rule to not joke around when someone is being serious. Often they will feel put down and you will come across as diminishing or negating the value of something they feel is very important, especially if they are sharing some very sincere feelings.

40. Be careful about how you use humor as it is very personal and subjective.

41. It is difficult to trust someone if what they want is to get somewhere as a result of having you in their life. When

someone has nothing to gain by your friendship chances are that they really like you for you.

42. People can only use the gifts and abilities they have to work with. Be aware. Don't put expectations upon people they cannot live up to.

43. Once, there was a person who told me, after she yelled at me, that she didn't feel the freedom to yell at just anyone. She meant it as a compliment and a measure that we were friends. Sorry, but friends like that I don't need.

44. A friend is a person you can count on to watch your back, not someone that you have to worry about stabbing you in the back.

45. The most important factor in having a good relationship is in choosing good candidates.

46. In American culture, when people don't get along, they are expected to always work it out. Other cultures often are more accepting that there are people who just don't get along.

47. Listen to what people want. They may not value the same things you do. So it's not, "Do unto others as you would have them do unto you," but rather, "Do unto others as *they* would have you do unto them."

48.   Listen to what people value because they will apply those same values to any relationship.

49.   Sometimes having much more knowledge than others is frustrating. Not only do you have fewer people to relate to, but you see things that they do not.

50.   If you hear someone bragging about how they gained by taking advantage of someone else, remember that usually only the names and faces change. You could be the person being taken advantage of in the next story.

51.   One way to assess people is to watch and listen to how they treat and value others. Don't think you're so special that they won't treat you the same way when it's convenient for them to do so.

52.   Information is likely to be biased when gathered by someone who has an emotional investment or interest in the results.

53.   Friendships are precious. Don't let the discomfort of resolving conflict stop you from repairing it.

54.   Don't get caught up on chronological age. It is not a measure of wisdom, youthfulness, energy level, ability to have fun, or ability to be understanding, caring, or nurturing. It simply means that one has been on the

planet for a certain period of time. It says very little about what one has done during that period of time.

55.   If you want to be in a relationship with a certain person, or type of person, then work on "being" the type of person they would be attracted to. Use this desire to work toward becoming a better person.

56.   The more emotionally needy you are the more likely you are to distort reality. So if you want a healthy relationship, work on being a healthy person. You will attract healthy people.

57.   To be easy to get along with, be accepting of the differences in others.

58.   Life works better when we set up circumstances and relationships that are compatible with who we are then. The key is in knowing who you are.

59.   People will go to all lengths to be loved and never consciously understand that wanting love is what drives them.

60.   "Do" love don't just "feel" love.

61.   Look for yourself in others. You will treat them better.

62. Listen to the crowd and you will soon be a part of the crowd—for better or worse.

63. Let people see who you are versus trying to sell yourself. Most people don't like to be pushed or pressured to buy something.

64. It's no fun to play with someone who always wins. Do you want playmates or do you want to validate your worth by putting down others?

65. If you want a good friend then you have to be a good friend.

66. Love built on appearance is like building a house in a riverbed in the middle of the summer; the rainy season is inevitable.

67. Love is in the doing not the saying.

68. Idealistic kindness: When one believes that people should always be kind to others even when they are harming themselves and/or others. You hurt others when you feed into this destructive behavior by not saying anything or just being polite which reinforces the behavior or attitude to continue.

69.   Sometimes it's best to love at a distance.

70.   In relationships, letting go of being right can keep your relationship right.

71.   "True" love is like a UFO . . . everyone has an opinion about it, but few have seen it and those that have don't know how to explain it to others in a way that makes it believable.

72.   See the person in the professional . . . It may help you make realistic expectations versus being distracted by the role or title.

73.   Sometimes the worst thing I can do is to do what "I think" another person needs rather than asking or listening to what they need.

74.   Forgiveness is not forgetting.   The situation may be: Now that I accept who you are and what you did without resentment, I see that I need more distance between us. I can forgive with the awareness you demonstrated that you are not a good candidate for a close relationship.

75.   Take people one at a time and you will see with more clarity who you are dealing with.

76. Truly caring about somebody means giving up some degree of freedom . . . you have to take into consideration how what you do affects others. You need to decide what your priorities are. Freedom versus emotional security is not without its trade-offs. What you choose will truly say what your real priorities are. You may be surprised and lonelier than you think.

77. Sometimes people need someone who will listen to their persistent complaints or frustrations. This is a one-sided relationship. You are a sounding board for people who want to talk about themselves.

78. Don't be a substitute for anybody. Be with people who see you as their first and only choice.

79. Don't mistake alliances for loyal friendship. The enemy of my enemy is my friend until we defeat our enemy, then my friend once again becomes my enemy.

    It's inconsistent to be against others being dishonest with you if you are dishonest with others. What's fair is fair. Which game do you want to play?

80. When someone is always judgmental of others when clearly there is no reason or evidence to support what he or she is saying, the problem lies within them.

81.   Study love. There are volumes on the different types. Most people seem to think that love is just a feeling.

82.   It's always better to leave them wanting more rather than having them wanting you to leave.

83.   In relationships men generally need only a few things to make them happy: Admiration. Approval. Affection.

84.   People often don't appreciate what or who they have in their life until it is lost and often it is impossible to get it back . . . that's unfortunate. But when one repeats this pattern over and over again . . . this is sad.

85.   When giving romantically, give a gift one wants rather than what one needs . . . Roses are much more romantic than tires.

86.   Nature is vested in *getting* people together not *keeping* people together. According to nature, a man's job is to spread his DNA. Only three percent of mammals mate for life according to the National Geographic channel.

87.   Some "I do's" last forever and some "I do's" last for short moments and some can't even bring themselves to say it. For each of these cases there are a thousand different reasons for their choices. Don't generalize as you will miss the uniqueness of individuals and the thousands

of different reasons that people do or don't do the same things.

88. Attraction versus love is often confused.

89. A safe relationship is when both partners have concluded that they have found the best they are capable of being.

90. Most people like the company of people who make them feel better as a result of their company.

91. With regard to relationships, it's not about the activity – it's about the company; when the activity matters more than the company, there might be something lacking with the company.

92. If you want a friend, you need to be a friend.

93. When you look to someone as your source of happiness it makes you crazy!

94. The perfect woman (man) is that fine line between being good enough and bad enough.

95. Violent people don't value discussion. Dishonest and greedy people don't respect contracts. Pay attention with your eyes and ears as to whom you are dealing with.

Don't make excuses for them and you will see clearer who they are. Then you can better decide where they fit into your life, if at all.

96. When I know your friends, I will know more about you.

97. Rather than trying to "get" someone, work on "getting to know" someone.

98. Our first experience in relationships is with our family. People transfer those same experiences, skills, and habits into their other relationships.

99. The more open you are to learning about yourself, the more open you are to learning about someone else.

100. The things people say give them away.

101. My father always said that "a wise man learns from other people rather than having to experience it all himself."

102. When your friend gets worried, he or she may take on a new personality, both in and how they are influenced, the fact that literally there is another person they need to take into consideration when choices are made. That new person may not be someone you would have chosen to spend time with if you had met them for the first

time. When one worries, it often changes their personal relationships.

In order to be comfortable with others, you must first be comfortable with yourself.

103. It is natural for new relationships to alter other existing relationships. After marriage each spouse will send and receive verbal and non-verbal communications and new agreements. As their marriage evolves, other relationships are likely to change.

104. The nicer people are, the better looking they get.

105. To be a person of integrity means standing up for others and for what's right even when you know ahead of time it's going to create personal hardships.

106. When people truly see the emperors of society and the clothes they profess to wear, they see how they've been misled.

107. People often like to *feel* like they're a good neighbor instead of *being* one.

108. Reliance has to do with what you "do" not what you "say" you'll do.

109. Be wary of people who brag and boast about how well they do at their profession and have little to show for their claimed accomplishments. Often people who brag are fooling themselves about their shortcomings and as a result others are also fooled.

110. Tell the truth when challenged and you won't have to remember the lie you made up.

CHAPTER 6

Truths

1. Often people act as mirrors to reflect back to us what
    we need to work on in order to become better people
    or to resolve issues we carry within. If you want to be
    liked, look for traits you like in others and try to emulate
    them until you can develop your unique way of doing
    something similar.

2. Your life is the only thing over which you truly have any
    degree of ownership. What are you going to do with it?
    It lasts a relatively short period of time. You may believe
    that you have control over others, but in reality it's only
    because they have allowed you the control.

3. He who has the best attorney wins; it is often not about who is in the right.

4. An example of a narcissist: Now that I've talked about me, let's talk about how you feel about me.

5. Opportunity may be disguised as crisis.

6. When one realizes for the first time that they are never going to have something they have always wanted, they will grieve, even though they never had it. They are grieving the loss of hope.

7. When one values appearance above all else, that's often all they get.

8. It is understandable but dysfunctional that people try to deflect the accountability for their mistakes onto others.

9. When I think that I am something I am not, I keep myself from seeing who I am, and from working on being the best I can.

10. If one was once perceived as being cool, but in fact was being unhealthy, even though one may be too old to be acting that way, the chances of the same behavior continuing are likely.

11. Too often wanting to feel better leads to avoidance. Dealing with what's needed in order to resolve personal issues leads to being healthier and feeling better. Change your priority to wanting to "be" better versus wanting to "feel" better.

12. We all want to "feel" significant. The best way to achieve this is to "be" significant. We all want to "feel" better. I suggest you focus on "being" better. The by-product of "being" better is "feeling" better in general.

13. When you have not seen somebody for a long time, leave some room for the idea that they may not be the same person you knew before. Otherwise, you may find yourself reacting to a distorted concept of someone rather than to the real person sitting in front of you. People make changes.

14. Don't get too caught up in achieving the end result of situations; rather, learn to recognize the value of the process.

15. Patience may be a virtue, however, that doesn't mean that you need to be patient with everything or everybody. Have no patience for dishonesty, lack of integrity, and issues that need to be dealt with promptly.

16. Life sometimes sucks, but it's better than the alternative.

17.   Alcohol mixed with conversation of opposing views is an explosion waiting to happen.

18.   Expectations are resentments waiting to happen.

19.   The best way to expose a traitor is to betray them. To not betray them is to support them.

20.   People tell you what they value, want, and fear by what they do (the choices they make). Allow people to tell you who they are by listening to the words they use and the choices they make.

21.   Often the real message is not in the literal statement or question, but rather in the implied message.

22.   Often what we are attracted to at first is the exact thing we wish would change later on.

23.   Money is only valuable because we have all agreed to treat it as such. Reality is that it's only paper with artwork. Honoring agreements can be powerful.

24.   Most people who are angry at groups of people are really only angry at a couple of significant people in their life.

25. Listen to the crowd and you will soon be a part of the crowd if you are not clear about who you are.

26. Just saying something over and over again doesn't make it valid. False statements remain false no matter how many times they are said or by how many people.

27. Jealousy is the banner of insecurity.

28. Intentions are like errands, you may end up with the same things but for different reasons. And, the way you feel about the things may change after you have heard the intentions.

29. In general, most people give respect when they think there is something to be gotten in return and a few people give respect because they have the wisdom to see that one has earned it.

30. If you feel entitled, chances are you are being rude. If you attempt to defend it, chances are you do this often.

31. How many pessimists are successful?

32. Equality is a concept that seldom applies to reality and will only be achieved when humans stop judging.

33. "You can't fix a problem with the same mind that created it." Work needs to be done to be able to think better and see more.

34. Tell the truth and you never have to worry about trying to remember what you have said.

35. Resolution comes with awareness and acceptance of the truth.

36. Anger is the reaction to not being able to control something you want to control. Or is a reaction to pain, hurt, or fear.

37. Opinion is the substitution for the truth which allows us to feel better.

38. Often degrees of truth lie in humor. Be careful when you use humor.

39. It's not always what you say but how you say it. A sarcastic tone of voice can be rude even when the literal words are not.

40. Always listen for even the smallest degree of the truth in what someone says. If the verbal feedback you receive has only one percent of truth or value, then be receptive

to that one percent. Over a lifetime, that adds up to a lot of knowledge.

41. Be vested in seeing the truth, not just getting your way, then you will see more.

42. Sex is the second strongest drive, only hunger is stronger. Be careful how you drive.

43. Sometimes letting go is the only way to move forward.

44. Some things cannot be unseen, unheard, undone. So, be careful what you say as it may be everlasting.

45. Sometimes people spread rumors to feel like they have some importance. What they need to do is to work on "being" more important rather than feeling more important.

46. In our society, cars are like skin. They tell others something about who is inside.

47. Arithmetic has no mercy and makes no error; any error is not in the math but rather in the person doing the math and such is life.

48. Reading psychology does not replace being in psychotherapy or counseling. Books do not make you confront the things you need to look at but are avoiding and often gives one the false belief that by being well read they have dealt with their issues when in reality they have not. So, they continue to be in denial of their issues and their unresolved issues continue to create problems. However, books are a good start to help facilitate growth.

49. When asked, "How old are you?" The man responded, "I'm old enough to know better and still young enough to sometimes do it anyway." He decided that his chronological age alone just wasn't an accurate presentation of him. By presenting a statement regarding who he is does have some relevance to his mental and emotional age and stage of development.

    Chronological age alone can be misleading. I have met youth with wisdom (although rare) and elderly with stupidity.

50. Maturity has much to do with the ability to control your impulses. Being civilized is a constant battle against the urges of nature.

51. It is not about "where" you are so much as it is about "who" you are wherever you go.

52. If you are holding a grudge over someone, you still have some more growing to do. This is not to be confused with choosing not to be in the company of someone that treats you with disrespect.

53. Difficult times provide not only an opportunity to become more in character but reveal what you have and don't have in character.

54. A good reputation leaves much room for error; be careful, reputations do change when people see repetition or patterns.

55. Doing things in extremes is usually a sign that something is wrong or needs to be addressed.

56. A story's ending is sad because the author quit telling the story. Try to remember that as long as you're alive, the story keeps going.

57. A person that wants nothing is independent and holds a position of strength. Coming from a position of wanting is coming from a position of weakness.

58. Alcohol at a young age can produce vitamin depletions that have irreversible effects leading to serious problems later in life, i.e., liver damage or Hepatitis C.

59.   Don't confuse someone who is helpful to you with someone who has become a crutch for you.

60.   If we allow others to think for us then what's the use of thinking at all.

61.   Greatness is a "clear desire" before it becomes a "reality."

62.   Some people talk to communicate and some people talk to manipulate.

63.   You are viewed by society based on what you do for society.

64.   Getting someone to understand one's position is extremely difficult when there is money to be made by not understanding.

65.   How can one much younger be equal when they haven't been on the planet long enough to do equal deeds. Equal is not a state of mind, it's a state of contribution and accomplishment.

66.   We do our young people and society a disservice when we encourage a casual first-name basis style of interacting to continue. A respectful society starts with practicing

good manners and acknowledging that just because you feel entitled doesn't mean that you are deserved.

67. The same flame that gives you warmth can also burn you.

68. A good roommate is one who is never home.

CHAPTER 7

Work

1. Romantic jobs are seldom financially rewarding; financially rewarding jobs are seldom romantic; having wealth can be pretty sexy.

2. The best career is one where the reward is in the work and not just in the paycheck.

3. When you go to work, work while you are there. Don't complain about how much work you have.

4. Focus on "your" work only, and not so much of the work of others. This will make you a better employee and a more likable coworker.

5. Work with people who have the same work ethic that you do and you will experience less conflict.

6. Nobody ever said while lying on their deathbed, "I wish I had worked more." Spend time with those that you care about. We do not last forever.

7. "I didn't seek out the profession; the profession sought me." When you can say this you probably are following your calling.

8. I notice that when I don't have to, then I do a better job. My choice has something to do with integrity and passion versus being told what to do.

9. The moment you begin to think seriously about retirement, you mentally retire in that moment.

10. After you die and it is said that, "He left his mark," ask yourself if you will be happy with the mark you left. If not, then get to work.

11. The moment you define your life based on material possessions is the moment you give up peace and contentment in your life. Real happiness is detached from material possessions. It doesn't mean that you don't enjoy them—just don't take them too seriously.

12. It's difficult to teach someone who thinks they have enough knowledge.

13. People who truly believe they are right and know more than others, cannot be receptive to new information. A closed mind has reached its potential.

14. Insecure people hide behind professional titles and their role.

15. "When you make choices, you live with them," is a famous saying. However, the real question is how well you live with your choices.

16. When you underdress at work, it doesn't look like you take your career seriously. And, it doesn't look like YOU want to be taken seriously.

CHAPTER 8

Spirituality

1.   In his last days the Pope refused to go to the hospital to be kept alive by man's technology. He wished to die with dignity and at the "time of God's choosing." Something for every person to think about.

2.   When one dances with the devil, he may get his feet stepped on.

3.   God creates them and then they get together.

4.   People want God to solve all their problems. What is needed is for each of us to look within ourselves to

discover the abilities God gave us to be able to handle our situations. Clarify what you need to work on to be a better, more competent person.

5.   When there is nothing that needs to be said, learn to be comfortable with silence. Silence can be a valuable place to get to know yourself.

6.   Live the life you like; like the life you live. But, for God's sake use some degree of good judgment and do what is needed to take care of yourself.

7.   It's what we do that defines us in society.

8.   Is God just an imaginary friend or is he/she/it the entity that is the all super power? Is God the reason for everything including disease and all things that feel good? Or is God so beyond anything any human is capable of understanding and, therefore, anything written about God is a feeble attempt to understand something we are incapable of understanding at all?

     When we die, we will know why we take chances. If you are going to be wrong, why not error on the side of contentment versus painful eternity. It's your choice. It's your life.

9. In a small house, God is everywhere; in a big house, God sometimes visits.

10. God seems to have designed a system by which we put ourselves in situations that reflect what we need to work on within ourselves. However, most resist this and prefer to focus on others which usually shows in the form of blame or anger. This removes the opportunity to grow and learn from the situation.

11. God is what God is; who am I to comment on the details?

12. Prayer is not to be used to get what you want. Use prayer to grow into more than you are and maybe you will get what you want from the growth. You may become more than who you are through the process.

13. Every situation is a story without an ending. In a moment when you don't get what you want, you may find some comfort in this phrase.

14. I have never met a person that doesn't have room for emotional, psychological, or spiritual growth. I believe even they would concede that the possibility for growth in certain areas of their lives is needed.

15.   For continued growth as a spiritual human being, replace the word "failure" with the phrase, "an opportunity to learn and grow." Don't get so attached to getting what you want. Don't run from emotional pain and discomfort. Provide time to have fun because fun is needed to recharge your battery so that you can cope with learning and growing.

16.   Exercise your brain, body, social skills, and spirit.

17.   Often less is more. Don't complicate your life with too much stuff. Often, it's all that stuff you worked so hard to get that gets in the way and keeps you stuck.

18.   It is suggested to prepare for old age based on how well the country you live in takes care of their elderly. Planning ahead might prevent the last days of your life from being helpless and uncomfortable.

19.   The moment we think that we finally know enough, God creates circumstances to let us know that there is still more to learn. And, sad to say, there are always people who just don't listen.

20.   Celebrate your skills by using them. When you can do something well, go do it. Enjoy your gifts and your life.

21. The difference between the saint and the sinner is that the saint has an invisible cloak of image.

22. People want God to solve all their problems rather than seeing what God wants us to learn as a result of having to deal with our problems.

23. The Bible says there is a time and a season for everything. Old age is a new season of life. What are you going to do with it?

24. If you believe there is some sort of a life after death, live your life consistently with that belief. If that is the case, it only makes sense to learn and grow as much as you can while you are alive on this planet. Then you'll have something to take with you.

25. Spend time by yourself and become aware of all your good qualities, then, put them to use. You'll feel good about yourself.

26. Be true to yourself and fair to others. Forget your regrets of the past. All that you give will return to you many times over.

27. Don't resent situations that bring discomfort. Remember, discomfort is where you learn and grow.

28. Money is not the root of all evil; it's the greed for money that causes people to lose perspective of the value of relations, fairness, and integrity. That's the root of all evil.

29. Faith is believing that things will turn out the way you want.

30. Anything seemingly good yet deceptive is a device of the Antichrist belief system.

31. Rather than focusing on and waiting for "the" Antichrist, look at yourself to see if you are acting like an Antichrist . . . being deceptive for personal gain at the expense of others.

32. Christ said, "Nobody knows when the end of the earth will be but the Father (God)." Matthew 24:36. So, focus on living.

CHAPTER 9

Moments

1.   Every moment has a purpose and an opportunity to learn
      something new.

2.   The moment you think about starting, you have started—
      just keep going.

3.   Work on seeing what God gave you to work with, then
      get to work. Understanding who you are is the first step
      to knowing what to do.

4.   Clarity about oneself is the road map to knowing what to
      do in your life.

5.   The way you see yourself affects how you interact with life and others.

6.   Your concept of yourself may be very different than who you really are. (Reality check yourself).

7.   Pay attention to what your body is telling you. It could save or prolong your life.

8.   The still person gathers more information.

9.   Be at ease with yourself. You are going to live with yourself always.

10.   Opportunities lie in things we complain about.

11.   Time is life and life is time; procrastination can lead to a wasteful life.

12.   Money magnifies what you want. Crisis clarifies who you are.

13.   When there is too much to do, it's sometimes best to sit and rest.

14. Moments don't last; they are moments. That's what moments do. So, all the more reason to savor, enjoy, appreciate, and truly live them.

15. Life is not one day at a time but one moment at a time. Just think of the thousands of moments you would miss if you lumped all the moments of the day together into a generalized day.

16. Where there is life, there is hope.

17. Your life is the only thing you have any degree of control over; so what are you going to do with it?

18. Remember, you can start over at any time.

19. Doing something fun doesn't resolve issues standing in the way of finding inner peace.

20. It is your life and it doesn't last forever, so spend your moments wisely. There is no guarantee that you will live to an old age.

21. You can see what you truly value by reviewing the choices you have made.

22. People often confuse wants with needs.

23. There is often a difference between feeling like you're good at something and actually being good at it. With practice and understanding of how you need to improve, you'll have both.

24. Avoid situations where your willpower will be tested when the possibility of failure leads to disaster.

25. We are all doing the best we can with what we have to work with from moment to moment.

26. Knowledge has a price, and sometimes the cost is that we don't get what we want.

27. Replace excuses with the question: "What's needed?" You'll keep yourself from getting stuck. "But" is a word that stops you from moving forward.

28. There are usually sacrifices when making changes.

29. There is a "need" we have that I have no name for, but the only way to get that need met is by helping others. One of the key elements to having a healthful, fulfilled life is to be open to the opportunities that help others.

30. Notice how much better you feel when you help someone.

31. Work hard to bring worth and value to society. Be proud of what you bring to the planet.

32. Don't make decisions in your life based on other people's judgments.

33. Take life too seriously and you'll create problems where there really were none.

34. Life doesn't wait for you to get back on your feet in order to move on.

35. The library is a brain bank. Get a library card.

36. There's some degree of sadness in all of us. There's also a degree of joy in all of us. There's some degree of every emotion in all of us. However, many of us are unaware of this fact until extreme events occur.

37. If you want to see a miracle, just look into the mirror. Then take a good look outside, it's all a miracle.

38. One's inside appearance often changes one's outward appearance.

39. To accomplish a desire is the sweetest fruit of all.

40. Following an excellent leader is no guarantee you will be led in the right direction. It could mean he or she is charismatic and good at getting people to follow them in a destructive direction.

41. Common sense is the lost Golden Rule.

42. You are unique! There is only one you. There has always been only one you, and there can only be one you. Therefore, you are priceless.

43. Nice things make life nicer when your inner life is in order.

44. A loving person thinks of love as having more to do with giving rather than feeling.

45. Having something to look forward to tends to brighten one's mood.

46. Be cordial or even helpful to people that get on your nerves, but be brief otherwise you will get sucked in.

47. Complete contentment and happiness are achieved with indifference to others' opinions and judgments.

48. People are similar to clothing. When you iron out the wrinkles in your life, you are more presentable.

49. Be clear about clarifying the truth.

50. Do today what makes you better for tomorrow.

51. Acting versus being: Be honest with yourself. Which one are you really doing?

52. Each moment will never be exactly the same again. A good reason to value each and every moment.

53. Any moment could be our last, so value every moment.

Contributions

➢ The stupid neither forgive nor forget. The naïve forgive and forget; the wise forgive but do not forget. *Sir Max Beerbohm* (1872 – 1956)

➢ If you want someone to stay with you, then be good company. As Steve Peltier says, people in relationships are like a wet bar of soap. If squeezed too tightly, it shoots from your hand.

➢ When you buy property, don't buy anything that you are not willing to live in yourself; you may need to someday. *Ray Hatherill*

➢ It's not what you say; it's how you say it. *Ray Hatherill*

➢ If you want people to enjoy your company and your conversation, get them to talk about themselves. They will walk away thinking what a great conversation they had and how nice it was to talk with you. *Ray Hatherill*

➢ Make excellence a habit and you create luck. "You are what you repeatedly do." *Greek Philosopher Aristotle*

➢ "The beauty of friendship is that it's all about choice." *Victor Felix*

About the Author

Dr. David Hatherill is a practicing psychotherapist, a Doctor of Clinical Psychology, Board Certified Diplomate with the International College of Professional Psychology and Prescribing Psychologists' Register, a licensed Marriage and Family Therapist, and Diplomate with the American Psychotherapy Association.

Dr. Hatherill's formal education and advanced studies are enhanced by his real-life experiences and excellent grasp of personality and family dynamics. In addition to extensive professional experience, he is world-traveled, speaks Portuguese as well as Spanish, and in the mid-nineties was an accomplished national recording artist and jazz guitarist.

His experience includes working in hospitals, private practice, clinics, expert witness court testimony, and lectures at colleges, universities, and other venues. He has pursued advanced studies and training with Integrating Spirituality Into Psychotherapy. Dr. Hatherill's practice includes the treatment of families, adults, and children.

Dr. Hatherill believes the profession of Psychotherapy is his calling and feels a strong commitment to help people by facilitating their emotional growth.

www.ingramcontent.com/pod-product-compliance
Lightning Source LLC
Chambersburg PA
CBHW020307290526
45784CB00003B/1395